WORKBOOK

THE GOOD LIFE

Lessons from the World's Longest Scientific Study of Happiness

A Guide To Robert J. Waldinger & Marc Shulz's Book

STUDY GENIUS

STUDY GENIUS PUBLISHING

DISCLAIMER:

The information provided within this book is for general informational/entertainment purposes only. While we try to keep the information upto-date and correct, there are no representations or warranties, express or implied, about the completeness, accuracy, reliability, suitability, or availability with respect to the information, products, services, or related graphics contained in this book for any purpose. Any use of this information is at your own risk.

YOUR FREE GIFT!

As a thank you for your purchase, we are giving

away 5 of our best selling workbooks *FOR FREE*!

Scan the QR code below to

download them now!

NOTE TO READERS:

This is a summary and analysis workbook based on The Good Life: Lessons from the World's Longest Scientific Study of Happiness by Robert Waldinger and Marc Schulz. It is meant to enhance your original experience, not replace it.

Scan the code below to

purchase the original book!

ABOUT THIS WORKBOOK

This workbook follows along closely as the lessons of The Harvard Study of Adult Development are described in detail throughout The Good Life.

There have been many lessons learned by the researchers throughout the study and this workbook will highlight the most impactful ones that will help you live a happier life. Throughout the book, there are many examples of conversations had with study participants over the years. These interviews shed light onto the lives lived and provide supporting evidence for the lessons learned about the importance of relationships.

Along with the main lessons in each individual chapter, there will also be journaling pages, discussion questions, activities, and more. These extra pages will ensure that the important research and lessons gleaned from The Harvard Study stay with you and become actions rather than just thoughts.

TABLE OF CONTENTS

Chapter One

What makes a good life?

*"We are always comparing our insides to other people's outsides." -
The Good Life, pg 2*

The good life is something we all want, something we all think we strive for, but the truth of it is that the good life is full of challenges and complications; it's full of love and pain. If we choose to only look at others or think that the good life is somewhere in the future, then we may begin to think that it is somehow always just out of reach. That is not true. The good life is something we can all have, but it is the process of living and throughout the unfolding of our lives is where we find happiness.

As the United States fought its way out of the Great Depression, the New Deal made way for projects such as Social Security and Unemployment Insurance. Alongside these new projects, there was a growing interest in learning what made people thrive. Not just what made people live a healthy life, but what made people *thrive*; what made people happy. Thus, a study at Harvard University began in 1938 and is still ongoing to this day. It has studied hundreds of individuals, starting with young men from Boston and following them throughout their lives. Eventually, some of their children were added to the study too. Throughout the study, these men were asked hundreds of questions, gave researchers access to medical records, and participated in countless interviews. All of the data has been continually studied and new results have been found to be true as time has passed.

The following is most important lesson researchers have learned and continue to see as true throughout the years:

Good relationships make people happier, and happier people are healthier.

Most people would agree that all they want in life is to "be happy," but people are also notoriously bad at knowing what is good for them. There may be the perfect choice right in front of you, but we usually think short term and therefore don't always choose our best option. Despite this flaw in our human nature, none of us are past the time of change. We all have the opportunity to make a change in our lives to start living happier and healthier by creating more quality connections with others around us.

IMPORTANT LESSONS

Key lessons from Chapter 1

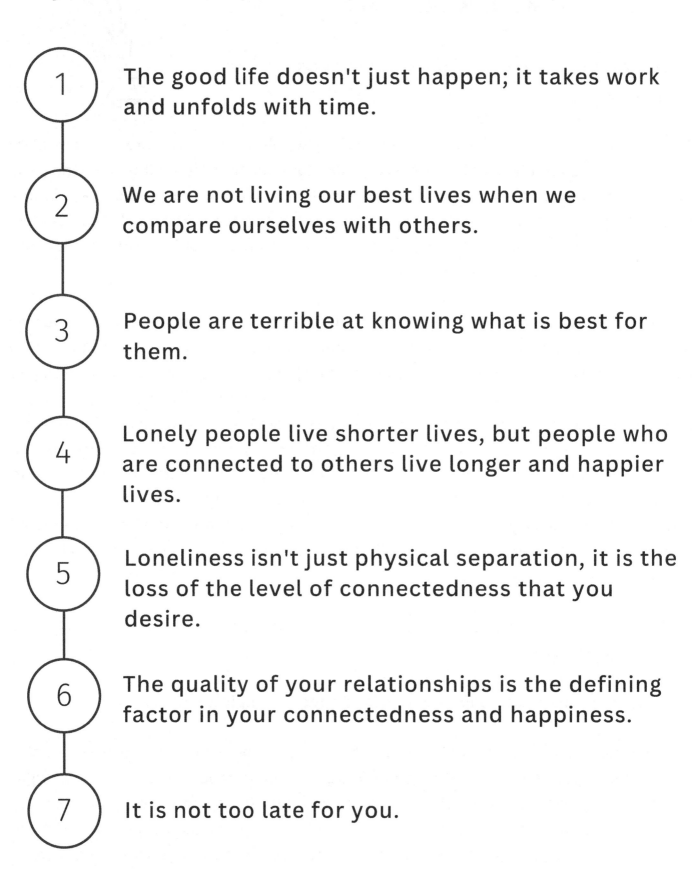

1. The good life doesn't just happen; it takes work and unfolds with time.

2. We are not living our best lives when we compare ourselves with others.

3. People are terrible at knowing what is best for them.

4. Lonely people live shorter lives, but people who are connected to others live longer and happier lives.

5. Loneliness isn't just physical separation, it is the loss of the level of connectedness that you desire.

6. The quality of your relationships is the defining factor in your connectedness and happiness.

7. It is not too late for you.

"The more you give to others, the greater your abundance." - Lao Tzu

How can you connect more with others? Who is someone in your life you would like to build a quality connection with?

Chapter Two

Why relationships matter

"Positive relationships are essential to human well-being." - The Good Life, pg 26

Humans have always relied on their instincts to survive. Even early humans knew how to respond when stress hormones or pleasurable feelings flowed through them. They knew to fight or flee or continue making a baby smile because it made them feel good. It is also known that early humans survived because they were social creatures. Living together eased the load, helped keep everyone protected, and allowed injured or elderly people to heal when hurt. Despite understanding that we are social creatures, many people struggle to find happiness and a sense of community. Now more than ever, loneliness is an increasing concern, but it is not too late to make meaningful changes.

There are 2 important truths to keep in mind while reading: the good life isn't always a major goal for people in developed societies, and we are often misled on our journey to find lasting happiness.

One major reason that we are misled on our quest for lasting happiness is due to the "spell of culture." Every culture that we are a part of is partially invisible to us; whether it is a larger city culture or even the culture in our individual homes. The culture we grow up in and live in influences the ideas we have about what will make us happy. This is typically why people think that money will make them happy. We refer to things like "getting a 'good' job" or "going to school to get a 'better' job." But both of these thoughts stem from our culture and ultimately rely on money being the key to happiness.

It is no secret that money can influence happiness, but understanding why is the key to understanding why we think that more money will make us happier. In a study done at Princeton University, researchers in 2010 found that $75,000 seemed to be a threshold amount for a family to start having all their basic needs met so they could focus more on their relationships and happiness. When people make less money, they can become stressed about how their basic needs will be met, but when those needs are met, they can focus on others around them instead of their struggles to survive.

IMPORTANT LESSONS

Key lessons from Chapter 2

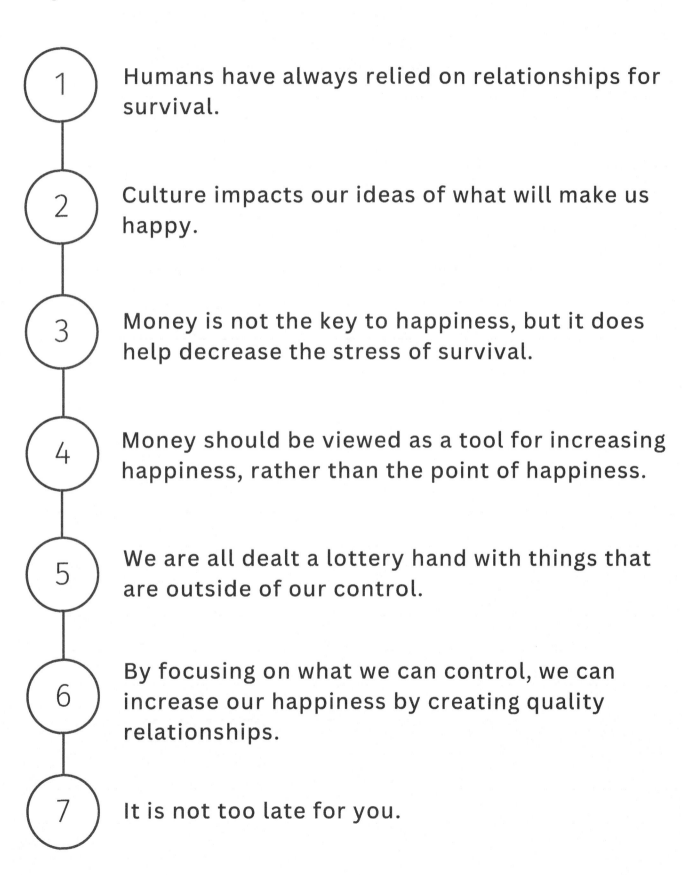

1. Humans have always relied on relationships for survival.

2. Culture impacts our ideas of what will make us happy.

3. Money is not the key to happiness, but it does help decrease the stress of survival.

4. Money should be viewed as a tool for increasing happiness, rather than the point of happiness.

5. We are all dealt a lottery hand with things that are outside of our control.

6. By focusing on what we can control, we can increase our happiness by creating quality relationships.

7. It is not too late for you.

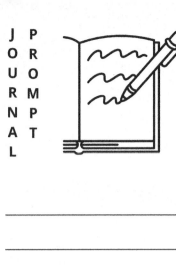

"Relationships are not just essential as stepping-stones to other things, and they are not simply a functional route to health and happiness. They are ends in themselves." - The Good Life, pg

Who can you build a better relationship with? How has your culture influenced your ideas of what happiness is?

_____

_____

_____

_____

_____

_____

_____

_____

_____

_____

_____

_____

_____

_____

_____

_____

_____

_____

_____

_____

_____

_____

_____

Chapter Three

Relationships on the Winding Road of Life

"No road is long with good company." - Turkish proverb

Life is a winding road that leads to new ups and new downs, no matter who you are or where you come from or how much money you make. The Harvard Study not only discovered a lot about the individuals, but also about how the patterns in their lives showed up in the lives of others around the world. As humans, we all share similar experiences. By understanding that we are all more alike than different, it becomes easier to empathize with those around you.

For years, the main focus of research on human development was done by studying children and how they grew up. Recently though, researchers have spent more time focusing on adults and how they change throughout their lives. The brain never stops developing and changing, meaning we all continue to grow despite passing the threshold into adulthood. Commonly, there are stages of life that are referred to when discussing development: adolescence, young adulthood, midlife, and late life. Based on these common stages, some people may feel that they are "on-time" or "off-time" in their development.

Whether you feel "on-time" or "off-time" is dependent upon what society thinks and what you expect of yourself. You can change your perspective on development and instead base your life on the relationships you create. Instead of going through the common stages, many people live through unexpected shocks which create unique stages in their life. These can stem from unexpected events, good or bad, and can lead to either good or bad things which will define a person's life.

By inviting more relationships into your life, you also invite chaos. But this is not a bad thing. Creating a support network can help you navigate these difficult times and help others when times are tough for them. Leaning into relationships can bring hurt, but it can also bring great joy to your life. It is through these important relationships that we can measure the progress, or stages, of our life.

IMPORTANT LESSONS

Key lessons from Chapter 3

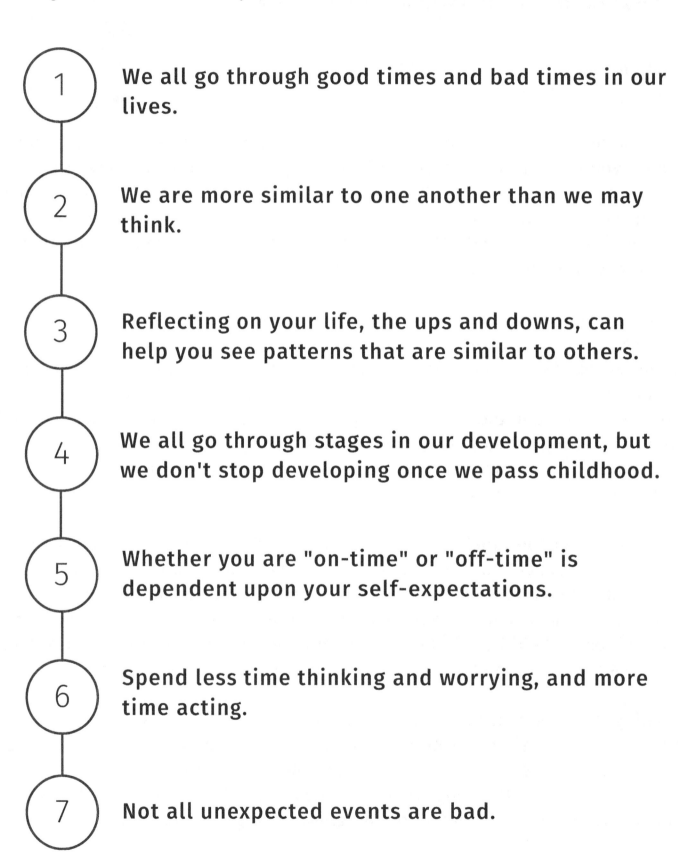

1. We all go through good times and bad times in our lives.

2. We are more similar to one another than we may think.

3. Reflecting on your life, the ups and downs, can help you see patterns that are similar to others.

4. We all go through stages in our development, but we don't stop developing once we pass childhood.

5. Whether you are "on-time" or "off-time" is dependent upon your self-expectations.

6. Spend less time thinking and worrying, and more time acting.

7. Not all unexpected events are bad.

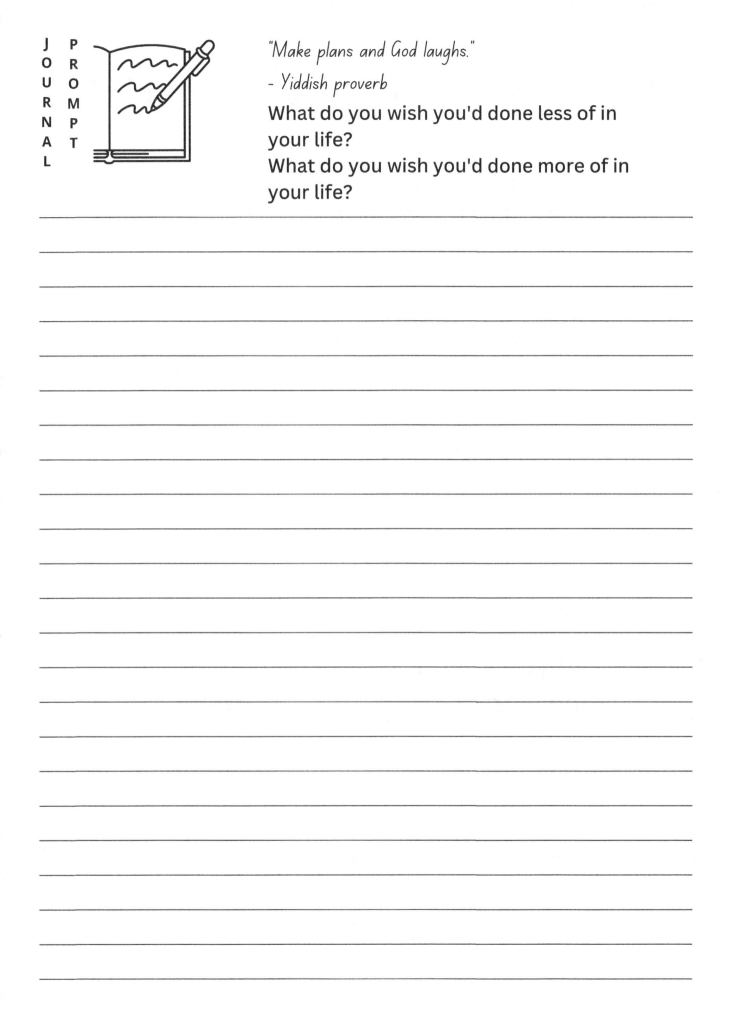

JOURNAL PROMPT

"Make plans and God laughs."

- Yiddish proverb

What do you wish you'd done less of in your life?

What do you wish you'd done more of in your life?

Mini-Harvard Study

Find an old picture of you when you were half your current age. Look at it, really look at it, and answer the following questions.

What were your hopes and dreams?

What were your worries and fears?

Who did you spend time with?

What were your plans?

Chapter Four

Social Fitness, Keeping Your Relationships in Good Shape

"The process of giving and receiving is the foundation of a meaningful life."
- The Good Life, pg 104

Most people understand that physical fitness is key to a healthy life, but not many people realize that social fitness is just as important. Our minds and bodies are inexplicably intertwined and exercising your relationships is just like exercising your muscles.

Being lonely has a physical effect on the body, making it more sensitive to pain, weakening the immune system, and causing diminished brain functionality. For older individuals, being lonely is twice as unhealthy as obesity and can increase the odds of an early death. Loneliness isn't defined by the amount of friends you have though; it is defined by the difference between the social interactions you have and the ones you want. The difficult part about loneliness is figuring out how to meet your relationship needs.

The best way to learn what your relationship needs are and how you can meet them is to reflect on the relationships you have right now. The next page has an activity that will help you discover the people in your life that you may want to spend more time with and how you can go about making that happen.

Joy comes from building connections with other people, and the best way to do that is to put in the effort. It doesn't have to be a monumental outreach though. Just like exercising, it takes time to build up muscles and social fitness will be no different. Get started building better connections with the people who are most important to you and then work from there at your own pace.

If you struggle with social fitness and feel awkward, try being radically curious. This means asking questions and being interested in the person you are talking to. Invest your time and energy into getting to know the people you care about and building a strong connection with them. These connections are what will bring us joy and help sustain us when times get tough. The relationships we build will be the key to our happiness and longevity.

IMPORTANT LESSONS

Key lessons from Chapter 4

1. Social fitness is just as important as physical fitness.

2. Self-reflection can help us learn what social muscles need work.

3. Being lonely has a negative physical affect on the body.

4. Focus on the people who energize you and bring joy into your life.

5. Build connections with radical curiosity and empathy.

6. Move your social muscles at your own pace.

7. The relationships we focus on will bring us happiness.

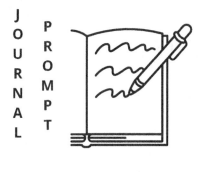

J O U R N A L   **P R O M P T**

"The frequency and the quality of our contact with other people are two major predictors of happiness." - The Good Life pg 95

Do you feel loneliness in your life? How do you practice social fitness?

Your Social Observatory

List the top 10 people in your life and think about the character of these relationships.

Who is in my life?	What is my relationship with them?	How does this relationship make me feel?
1		
2		
3		
4		
5		
6		
8		
7		
9		
10		

Whom do I want to have a better relationship with?

Keystones of Relationships

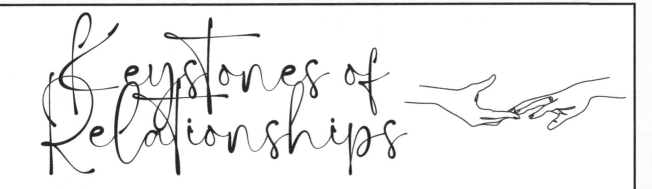

SAFETY
Who would you call if you woke up at night and were scared?

SECURITY
Who would you turn to in a moment of crisis?

LEARNING
Who encourages you to try new things?

GROWTH
Who supports you in pursuing your life's goals?

CLOSENESS
Who knows almost everything about you?

CONFIDING
Who can you ask for advice?

IDENTITY AFFIRMATION
Who strengthens your sense of who you are?

SHARED EXPERIENCE
Who has shared many experiences with you?

INTIMACY
Do you feel satisfied with the amount of intimacy in your life?

HELP
Who do you turn to if you need help solving a practical problem?

FUN
Who makes you laugh and is always invited when you go out?

RELAXATION
Who makes you feel relaxed and at ease?

Chapter Five

Attention to Relationships

"Time and attention are not something we can replenish. They are what our life is. When we offer our time and attention, we are not merely spending and paying. We are giving our lives." - The Good Life, pg 119

One day, we will all run out of time. If you could see the grains of sand in your hourglass falling away, would that change how you live your life? Would you focus less on some things and more on others? These are the questions we must grapple with because it is a fact that we all have an end date.

With this in mind, we need to move forward with thoughtfulness in how we spend our time. Attention is love in its most basic form, yet how often do we give someone our full attention? Typically, our minds wander to think about things that have happened or things that have not yet happened. The inability to stay completely focused wastes our brains energy and time. And yet, we allow our minds to wander when we should be focused on the relationships we are building or the people we are talking to or simply the present moment.

Mindfulness is the act of being present. You can practice mindfulness when speaking to others or when sitting at home alone. Focusing on what is going on in the present moment, like what is happening around you or what another person is saying, can help you give your full attention instead of being distracted by the past or future.

While technology and social media have helped a lot of people connect with others, especially during the pandemic, they can also have negative effects if used incorrectly. A human interaction can't be duplicated by a machine; therefore, it is best to use technology to connect with others and enhance the good in the world instead of using it as a simple distraction. There are a few recommendations on the following pages for how to use technology and social media to enhance the good in our lives.

Relationships are hard, no matter if we are physically together or miles apart. While being present all the time is nearly impossible, it is the effort that is important. It is more important to be there for others and try to understand them by being curious than it is to be right or superior in some way. Ask yourself what actions you can take to give attention to someone in your life who deserves it.

IMPORTANT LESSONS

Key lessons from Chapter 5

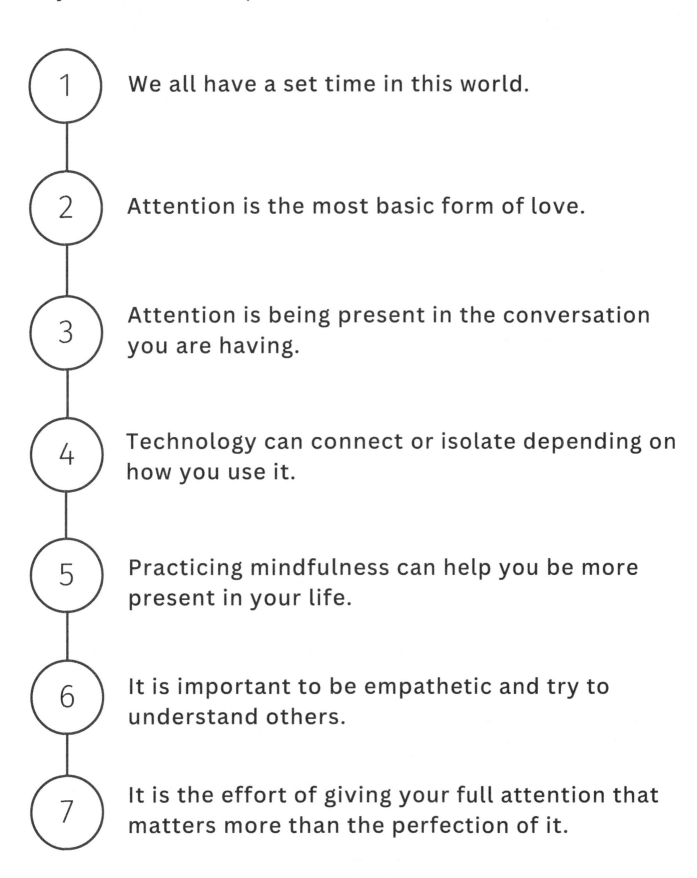

1. We all have a set time in this world.

2. Attention is the most basic form of love.

3. Attention is being present in the conversation you are having.

4. Technology can connect or isolate depending on how you use it.

5. Practicing mindfulness can help you be more present in your life.

6. It is important to be empathetic and try to understand others.

7. It is the effort of giving your full attention that matters more than the perfection of it.

JOURNAL PROMPT

"Attention is the most basic form of love."
- John Tarrant

Who gets the most of your attention?
Who deserves more of your attention?

Recommendations for using social media

How can we use social media for good? These 4 recommendations can help you mitigate the negative effects of using social media and instead use it to connect and build strong relationships.

Don't just scroll; engage with others on their posts or pictures. Building these connections can help you build stronger relationships.

Remember: don't compare yourself to what you see on social media.

Take your temperature when using social media and ask yourself how you feel when using it and after using it. Does social media scrolling make you feel better or worse?

Remember: self-reflection can sometimes be a harsh critic.

Check-in with how your social media use is seen by other people around you. Are you spending more time on social media than you are with your partner?

Remember: don't compromise your relationships based on what you see on social media.

Take tech holidays once in a while and disconnect from everything online. When we feel so connected, it's sometimes hard to see how disconnected we really are.

Remember: be present.

Mandala

A coloring page to use while practicing mindfulness.

Chapter Six

Facing the Music

"There are two pillars of happiness revealed by the Harvard Study... one is love. The other is finding a way of coping with life that does not push love away." - George Vaillant, The Good Life pg 140

We will all face countless challenges in our lives; some will define us and force us to change. No matter what these challenges might be, we all have a choice. We can either turn away from the pain out of fear and hide, or we can face things head on and work through them. The Harvard Study showed that individuals who avoided challenges and talking about life's difficult times experienced negative effects on their health over the next 30 years.

Strong relationships also bring tough challenges because the people we love the most can also hurt us the most. We can make the choice to hide our issues and true selves from our loved ones to keep ourselves safe, or we can choose vulnerability and deepen our connection with them despite the risks. By creating these deeper connections, we not only invite joy and happiness into our lives, but we also increase our overall health. To get to this place of vulnerability and connectedness, we need to understand why we fear deep connections in the first place.

All of us grow up in particular environments that affect how we think and act, creating ingrained habits that can be hard to shake. Sometimes, we may also experience a life-changing event that can cause us to create a new habit that will impact future relationships. These reflexive behaviors can keep us stuck in a cycle that does not bring us the happiness we deserve. To break this cycle and these habits, you can try using the W.I.S.E.R. model which helps with self-reflection. This model will be detailed on the following page.

Using the W.I.S.E.R. model, we can take a step back, look at our situation from an outside perspective, and consciously choose how to react instead of letting our old habits define what we do. When using this model, it is important to pay attention to your emotions. When you feel deep emotions, it means that something is going on inside of you that needs to be examined. Take the time to look and dig into how you feel so that you can be vulnerable and share your ups and downs with those around you.

IMPORTANT LESSONS
Key lessons from Chapter 6

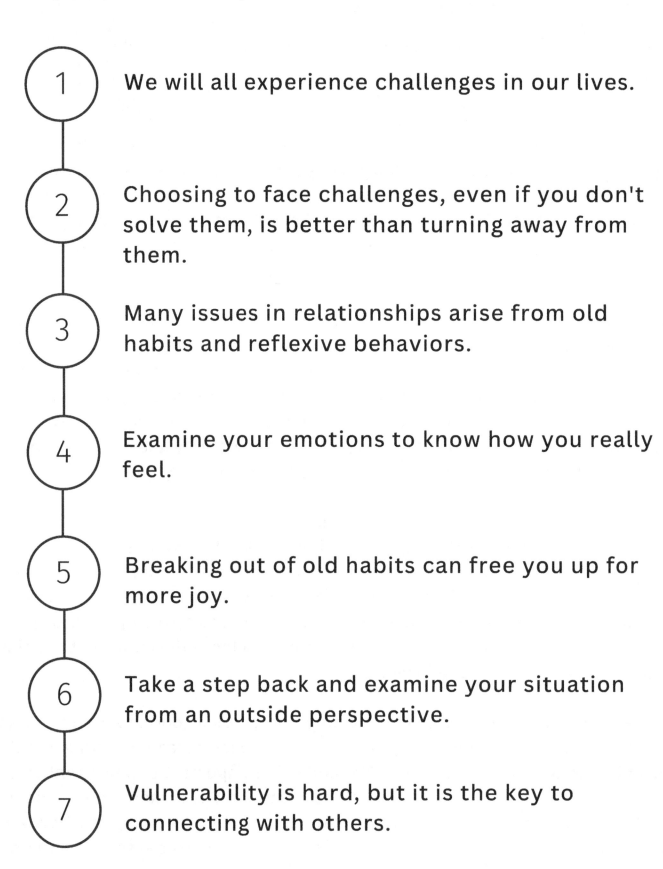

1. We will all experience challenges in our lives.

2. Choosing to face challenges, even if you don't solve them, is better than turning away from them.

3. Many issues in relationships arise from old habits and reflexive behaviors.

4. Examine your emotions to know how you really feel.

5. Breaking out of old habits can free you up for more joy.

6. Take a step back and examine your situation from an outside perspective.

7. Vulnerability is hard, but it is the key to connecting with others.

"The world we live in is the world we create."
- Shohaku Okumura

When you are faced with a challenge, do
you turn away or face it head-on?
How can you listen to your emotions
better in difficult situations?

W.I.S.E.R Model

W

Watch
Initial impressions are very powerful, but they are also rarely complete or accurate. Be radically curious about what is going on around you and within you.

I

Interpret
Understand the situation and the reality of it. Your emotions will tell you if there is something more important going on that you may not know about.

S

Select
Choose what you should do rather than reacting. Think through what your goals are for the situation and what resources you have at your disposal.

E

Engage
Engage the strategy that you have selected and watch carefully how all parties react, including yourself.

R

Reflect
Take time to reflect and think about how the situation went. Was the issue resolved? Did you learn something?

Chapter Seven

The Person Beside You

"Love is the name for our pursuit of wholeness, for our desire to be complete." - Plato

There is no universal formula for love or singular way to be right when it comes to finding the right person for you. Intimate connections change from culture to culture, generation to generation, and person to person. We are influenced by how we grow up and the experiences we have as adults, but ultimately, our love story will be completely unique to us.

Like other relationships, love is hard because we open ourselves up to the possibility of getting hurt. Intimacy comes with great risk to ourselves, but we still all long for the security, safety, and care that a loved one can give to us. There is a lot of research that has been done on intimate relationships, both for children needing care from a parent and for adults needing support from a partner. One study even showed that holding the hand of a loved one can reduce stress and act as a mild anesthetic during medical procedures.

Alongside our intimate relationships come intense emotions. These emotions can cause great happiness or conflict. It's no secret that even happy relationships have their good and bad times, but the Harvard Study found it is how conflicts are resolved that matters most. As in the previous chapter, some in the study chose to turn away from their feelings and the challenge in the relationship while others turned toward it and became vulnerable to work things out. The couples who spent time being vulnerable, listening to each other, and showing empathy found greater happiness in their lives. Hardships usually arise from our internalized reactions that are controlled by our fears. If we let our fears control us, then the things we fear most will become our reality.

For early humans, relationships were created out of necessity for survival. For us now, our relationships are still driven by that need for human connection, but it is up to us to tend to them. We no longer need others for survival, so our relationships take more effort to maintain. Like plants, relationships need attention and nourishment if they are to thrive and bring us joy. It is not to late to change how you tend to your relationships—especially your intimate ones.

IMPORTANT LESSONS

Key lessons from Chapter 7

1. Love is unique, just like us.

2. Having an intimate relationship with someone means opening yourself up to risk.

3. Research has shown the numerous health benefits of having an intimate relationship.

4. Disagreements arise from internalized fears and anxieties that have been bottled up.

5. During disagreements, practice vulnerability, active listening, and empathy.

6. Relationships need attention and nourishment if they are to thrive.

7. It is not too late to change how you interact in your intimate relationships.

JOURNAL PROMPT

"To be alive is to be vulnerable."
- Madeleine L'Engle

When was the last time you were vulnerable with your partner?
How can you be more vulnerable in your relationships?

_____

_____

_____

_____

_____

_____

_____

_____

_____

_____

_____

_____

_____

_____

_____

_____

_____

_____

_____

_____

Relationships are like plants; they need tending.

Chapter Eight

Family Matters

"Call it a clan, call it a network, call it a tribe, call it a family: Whatever you call it, whoever you are, you need one." - Jane Howard

Our families are a part of who we are and are typically a defining factor in the way that we choose to live our lives. But just because we were raised a certain way in a certain household with certain rules, does not mean we have to continue living that way if it does not serve us. These social inheritances that we carry with us can present themselves in negative or positive ways. Learning what these inheritances are and breaking the old habits we have can help us build stronger relationships and bring more joy into our lives.

What we experience during childhood is incredibly important. Many researchers have studied childhood development, particularly in relation to family dynamics, and have found that a negative experience can cause serious developmental issues later on in life. Studies have also found that if a child has one person in their life who shows them love and believes in them then, despite their household life, the child can grow up into a normal adult. Having a healthy childhood can teach us how to manage our emotions and learn to connect with people to build strong relationships as adults.

There are also instances where someone decides to choose their own family. This will typically happen to ostracized people, such as LGBTQ+ individuals, who do not seem to fit into their biological family. Families come in all shapes and sizes, which means that it does not matter if you choose your family later in life or if you are born into one that seems to fit you. The most important thing to remember about family is to build strong connections and lean on those connections when you need to. Whether this be with your biological mother, adopted father, chosen sister, or brother-in-law, family is important and we all need one.

The Harvard Study showed that no matter the upbringing of a child, the future is not set in stone for anyone. There are always opportunities for change, even at later ages. This means that even if you struggled as a child or struggle as an adult, there is still time for you to make changes in your life. Unlearning and relearning can help you identify old behavior patterns, break negative social inheritances, and create strong connections with new people.

IMPORTANT LESSONS

Key lessons from Chapter 8

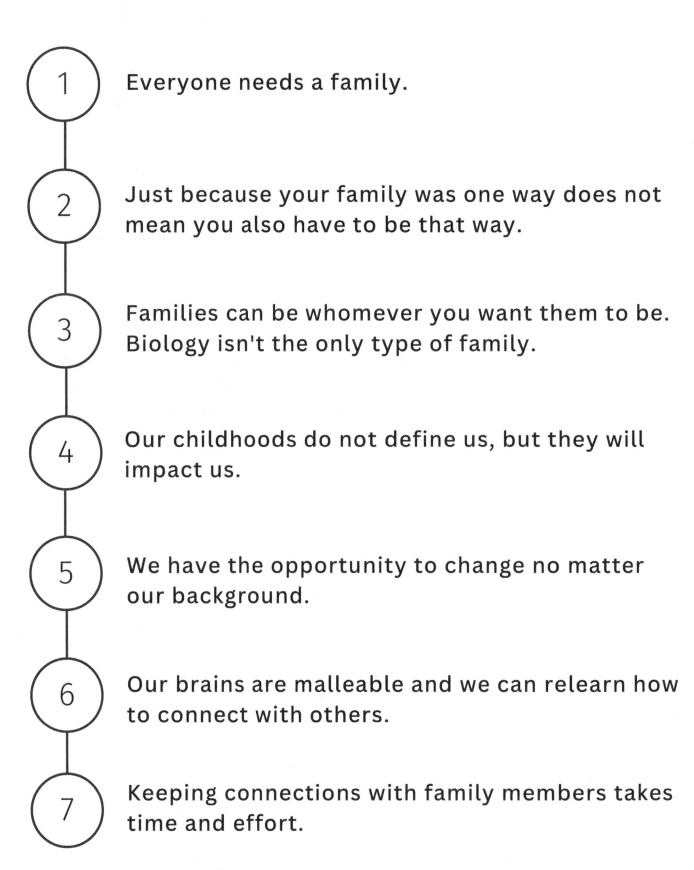

1. Everyone needs a family.

2. Just because your family was one way does not mean you also have to be that way.

3. Families can be whomever you want them to be. Biology isn't the only type of family.

4. Our childhoods do not define us, but they will impact us.

5. We have the opportunity to change no matter our background.

6. Our brains are malleable and we can relearn how to connect with others.

7. Keeping connections with family members takes time and effort.

J O U R N A L   P R O M P T

"How a family adapts to that inevitable change is one of the key determinants of the quality of family relationships." - The Good Life, pg 198

How did your childhood impact you?
Do you have strong family connections?

_____

_____

_____

_____

_____

_____

_____

_____

_____

_____

_____

_____

_____

_____

_____

_____

_____

_____

_____

_____

_____

_____

_____

Steps to change

Turn toward difficult feelings instead of ignoring them.

Try to catch other people behaving well in relationships.

Remain open to people behaving differently than you expect.

Notice when you are having more positive experiences than you expected.

Start with yourself.

Routines are important.

Put in the effort to keep connections.

Chapter Nine

The Good Life at Work

"Research has shown that people who have a best friend at work are more engaged than those who don't." - The Good Life, pg 235

A majority of our lives will be spent working. Whether you work to put food on the table or because you love the job you do, work is still a large part of our lives. Since it is a large part of our lives, there will always be overlap between our work lives and our personal lives, despite our best efforts. But our two lives do not have to be exclusive. By building quality relationships with the people we work with, the job can become easier and more enjoyable, leaving us happier when we get home. Instead of looking at the two as separate, think of your life in terms of the relationships you have and divide your attention accordingly.

The Harvard Study found that the people who did not build relationships at their work were overall less happy than those who did. Another study found that stress from work is often taken home and released on those we love most, despite our best efforts. And another study by Gallup found that quality relationships at work actually increased productivity and overall employee happiness. Each of these studies points to the fact that relationships at work can help us lower our stress, increase our happiness while at work, and increase our happiness when we get home.

Work is a major source of socialization and connection. Whether it be with our coworkers, managers, or customers, we are around people who we can build connections with. These connections can keep loneliness in the workplace at bay and leave us feeling more fulfilled in our jobs. Unfortunately, being around others at work has changed drastically with the COVID-19 pandemic. Now, more people are working from home and missing out on those crucial connections that are typically made in the office.

Instead of sitting by and letting old relationships die or avoiding making new ones, try practicing social fitness and finding other ways to connect with people. You can connect online, join a group at your local gym, or get coworkers from your office together to go bowling. No matter what you do, do not let the crucial relationships built at work, the ones that bring your job joy, fade away.

IMPORTANT LESSONS

Key lessons from Chapter 9

1. Your job does not always indicate your level of happiness.

2. Our personal and work lives are not as separate as we think they are.

3. Most people bring the stresses of work home with them each day.

4. Friendships in the workplace can increase joy and productivity.

5. We spend most of our lives at work and it is a major source of socialization.

6. The pandemic has changed how we work and caused loneliness for a lot of people.

7. It is not too late to reach out and connect with your coworkers.

J O U R N A L
P R O M P T

"Change the nature of work, and you change the nature of life." - The Good Life pg 244

Do you have close relationships at work? How has the pandemic changed your workplace relationships?

Questions to ask yourself about your workplace relationships

Who is my closest friend at work?

What do I appreciate about the people I work with?

Who is different from me and what can I learn from them?

Can I use the W.I.S.E.R. model with someone who is making me upset?

What connections am I missing at work?

Do I really know my workmates?

Chapter Ten

All Friends Have Benefits

"Without friends, no one would choose to live." - Aristotle, Nicomachean Ethics

As kids, friendships are absolutely integral to our lives and it is very easy to choose a best friend. But as adults, we seem to let friendships fall to the wayside and sometimes have a hard time choosing who our best friend is due to a lack of strong connections. Entering into adulthood brings a lot of additional responsibilities, and we typically choose to place our friendships behind things like work and family. While this may seem like a logical choice, it is one that will inevitably bring us less happiness.

Friends help with a lot of things, whether it's moving, moral support, or stress relief, they have our backs through good times and bad. Not only that, but having strong friendships also increases life expectancy. As we age, our friends change and we find that we relate to certain people more as we go through different stages of life together. While there is no set amount of friendships you should have to increase your life expectancy, you should think about your friends regularly. Think about who you have talked to recently or who you haven't spoken to in a long time. Which friendships are growing cold and what can you do about them? The strongest friendships flow both ways.

While the Harvard Study focused primarily on men, they did expand their interviews to include some of the participants' wives. They asked each couple about their friendships and found that most of the men had fewer friends than the women did. When asked why, the men commonly said that they were self-sufficient and independent, not needing anybody to lean on. There were also a few who had many friends and spoke very highly of how often they connected with them and leaned on each other. This mentality of not being a burden to someone and not keeping in contact with them to maintain your friendship is a typical generational social inheritance. Friendships are easy to neglect; with tending, they can continue to flourish. We can break old patterns of thought, learn that we are not a burden to our friends, and build strong connections with those we have neglected. No one is past the point of changing.

IMPORTANT LESSONS

Key lessons from Chapter 10

1. Friendships give us life.

2. Adults need friends just as much as kids do.

3. We can be independent and self-sufficient, and still have friends.

4. We are not a burden to our friends.

5. Even a friendly moment with a stranger can bring us joy.

6. Casual friendships are still good relationships.

7. It is not too late to make new friends or connect with old ones.

JOURNAL PROMPT

"What is my object in making a friend? To have someone to be able to die for, someone I may follow into exile." - Seneca

Who are your friends?
What makes your relationship with these people so strong?

_____

_____

_____

_____

_____

_____

_____

_____

_____

_____

_____

_____

_____

_____

_____

_____

_____

_____

_____

_____

Conclusion

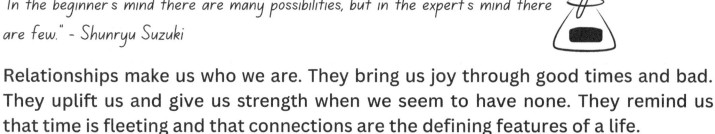

It's Never Too Late to be Happy

"In the beginner's mind there are many possibilities, but in the expert's mind there are few." - Shunryu Suzuki

Relationships make us who we are. They bring us joy through good times and bad. They uplift us and give us strength when we seem to have none. They remind us that time is fleeting and that connections are the defining features of a life.

Whether you have many friends, few friends, great connections, or weak ones, it is not too late to make changes in your life. Start small, invite some quality people into your life, and be vulnerable with them. Be radically curious about someone you don't know very well. Talk to a complete stranger while waiting in line. The time to change is right now.

It is never too late.

Thank you!

Study Genius is a collective of students, writers, editors, designers, and researchers that strive to create the best summary books and workbooks on the market.

We would like to thank you for helping us support our passions. We hope you learned new and exciting information from this book that will carry on into your daily lives.

If you enjoyed this book, would you please leave us a five-star review? It will help us to continue to publish books and take care of our collective business.

Made in the USA
Las Vegas, NV
10 September 2023

77413427R00026